Easy Activities, Prayers , and Projects for Children

Bundles of Faith and Tons of Fun

Patricia Mathson

ave maria press   Notre Dame, IN

© 2000 by Ave Maria Press, Inc.
All rights reserved. No part of this book may be used or reproduced in any manner whatsoever, except in the case of reprints in the context of reviews, without written permission from Ave Maria Press, Inc., P.O. Box 428, Notre Dame, IN 46556.
International Standard Book Number: 0-87793-942-X
Cover design by Brian C. Conley
Text design by Brian C. Conley
Printed and bound in the United States of America.

Library of Congress Cataloging-in-Publication Data

Mathson, Patricia L.
    Bundles of faith and tons of fun : easy activities, prayers, and
        projects for children / Patricia Mathson.
            p. cm.
Includes bibliographical references.
        ISBN 0-87793-942-X (pbk.)
        1.Christian education of children. 2. Christian education—
Teaching methods. I. Title.
BV1475.2 .M367 2000
268'.432--dc21
                                                                00-008521
                                                                CIP

This book is dedicated to
my husband,
Dick,
and our children,
Cathy and Steve.

Contents

Introduction

Children are the future of our church. This is a book full of ideas for those who want to share their faith with the next generation. *Bundles of Faith and Tons of Fun* includes activities, crafts, and prayers that encourage children to grow in their faith and explore more deeply what it means to be a follower of Jesus Christ. Catechists, teachers, parents, and all those who work with children can use this book to help those who are learning to walk with Jesus to be people of hope in our world today. We are all on a journey of faith with Jesus to the Father with the help of the Holy Spirit.

Any form of effective religious education requires a variety of methods and approaches. *Bundles of Faith and Tons of Fun* is designed to provide help in that area. Each of the chapters offers specific lessons and several ways to enhance a course. The activities are organized by chapters under important themes, topics, and seasons of the church that all go into our faith journey.

Organization of the Book

Prayer is crucial for children to be able to cultivate a personal relationship with Jesus. We pray not only for our needs, but for the needs of others. In Chapter 1, "Inviting Children to Pray," the activities are intended to help children pray both in their own words and through traditional prayers.

We are called to live in *peace and justice* as followers of Jesus Christ. We are to work for the rights of all people—especially the most vulnerable—under our constant realization that all people are created in God's image and likeness. Chapter 2 provides learning activities to help children learn to reach out to others in Jesus' name.

The *Bible* is the book of the church. The word of God speaks to our contemporary lives. We are called to live gospel values each day. Familiarity with Bible stories is both enjoyed by children and a necessity for their faith lives. It is important for children to know how scripture stories speak to their hearts and their lives. Activities in Chapter 3 are designed to help the students know, appreciate, and pray with the Bible.

The *seasons of the church year* offer a tangible way for children to learn important lessons of faith. The journey of faith theme is emphasized clearly in Chapters 4 and 5, "Welcoming Advent and Christmas" and "Walking through Lent and Easter." Also, in Chapter 6, "Celebrating Special Days," activities, prayers, blessings, and role-play are offered to help the children explore holidays and special feasts along the way.

Who Can Use This Book

The material in this book can be used in a variety of ways and in a number of different religious education settings. The material can be used in parish religious education programs, Catholic school classrooms, summer programs or Bible camps, parish liturgies and activities, after school programs, family events, sacramental preparation times, and at home. The activities can be used with students in preschool, elementary, and middle school age groups.

While most of the material requires a minimum of preparation and extra materials, it is wise to do a thorough study of the entire chapter during your initial preparation time for the course or unit. Preview all of the activities. Jot down notes to help you to remember when a particular activity or exercise may be most appropriate. Collect supplies. Schedule the exercise or activity in your plan book.

Hopefully this book will lead to other ideas and other activities. Each catechist must adapt the activities presented to his or her learning situation. Each age group is different, each class is different, and each catechist is different. Activities must be selected, organized, and presented so that they are meaningful to the group with whom they are used. The catechist must look for ways to share the faith in concrete ways that children can understand and may find exciting.

The pages that follow offer many approaches under the various themes for the religious education of children.

1

Inviting Children to Pray

Prayer connects us with God's presence in our lives and helps us build a relationship with God. Prayer is an important part of our faith journey with Jesus. Prayer makes us one with God, our Father and Creator, through the help of the Holy Spirit.

It is very important to help children learn to pray in many ways. Children have different personalities, backgrounds, and interests; they should be taught how to pray individually. In this way they can share with God what is in their hearts and minds. Prayer helps children understand that God is always with us.

It is also important to help the children learn to pray traditional prayers. These prayers are passed on from generation to generation. The words of traditional prayers also help us express what we believe. Traditional prayers remind us that we are dependent on God for all things and in all ways.

Prayer reminds us of who we are as God's people and who we are called to be. We must not only stress the importance of prayer to the children, but show it by example. Prayer must be a part of each gathering with children. We must also remember to pray for the children in our care, both in our personal prayer and communally with others. This chapter offers many suggestions for encouraging new ways to pray and enhancing ways that are already taking place.

Prayer Table

A prayer table in the classroom helps children focus on praying to God. A prayer table should always have a bible on it. The bible can be opened to a scripture reading appropriate to the season or the lesson.

Also, the prayer table can be changed for each liturgical season by changing the color of the cloth and the items displayed. A piece of felt can be cut for the center of the prayer table in violet for Advent and Lent, white for Christmas and Easter, and green for ordinary time.

Items appropriate to the season include a dish of ashes or a cactus for Lent, a crown of thorns for Holy Week, a bowl of holy water or a butterfly picture for Easter, an Advent wreath for Advent, and a nativity scene for Christmas.

For ordinary time a green plant or a basket holding the petitions the children have written can be displayed. If possible hang a cross over the prayer table.

A candle can be displayed in any season to represent Jesus as the light of the world. The candle should be lit, however, only when children are actually gathered around the table for prayer.

Gather the children in front of the prayer table for prayer at the beginning or end of class.

Class Discussion on Prayer

Talk about prayer in your class. A class discussion helps broaden the children's concept of where, when, and how we pray to God. Here are some questions to ask the children about prayer:

Why do we pray?

What is your favorite prayer?

What kind of prayer do you pray in the morning?

When are other times we can pray?

Who are people that need our prayers?

What are some places where we can pray?

When do you pray most often—when you are sad? happy? afraid?

How do you pray before meals?

What are your own words you use to pray to God?

What are some things you thank God for in prayer?

These questions encourage the children to talk about prayer. Let several children give an answer to each question. Ask the children to listen to the responses of the other children. In this way the children can learn about prayer from one another.

Prayer Intention Cards

An important part of teaching children about prayer is to help them understand that we should pray not only for our needs, but the needs of other people.

Discuss with the students the many people in our world who need our prayers and our responsibility to pray for them. Some children are aware of people for whom we should regularly pray. Other children may not realize that some people go to bed hungry at night or that everyone does not have a warm place to sleep.

Praying for other people unites us with them. It reminds us of our common identity as the people of God. Prayer also helps each of us be aware of what is really important in life.

Have each child fill out a prayer intention card to help them learn to pray for others. Prayer intention cards are easily made by creating a form on a half sheet of paper and copying it before class for each child. The form can go like this:

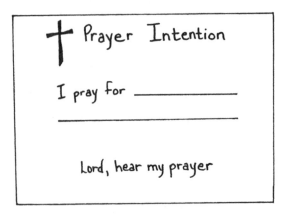

Prayer cards can be duplicated on white paper or on a color appropriate to the season of the church year. The children can fill out one prayer intention card or several. Have the children place the completed prayer intention cards in a wicker basket. Have them brought forward during a prayer service or placed on the class prayer table. Leave extra cards out so the children can add more prayer intentions to the basket at a later time.

Scripture Verses

Jesus showed us by his words and example that prayer is important. Jesus prayed before choosing his apostles, he prayed before accepting the challenge of the cross, and he taught his apostles to pray. The early Christians sought to be people of prayer like Jesus.

Assemble the students into small groups. Give each student a bible and the scripture citations listed below. Ask the children to look up the verses in the bible. Then call on students to share what each verse means.

Acts 2:42	They devoted themselves to the teaching of the apostles and to the communal life, to the breaking of the bread and to the prayers.
Philippians 4:6	Have no anxiety at all, but in everything, by prayer and petition, with thanksgiving, make your requests known to God.
1 Thessalonians 5:17-18	Pray without ceasing. In all circumstances give thanks, for this is the will of God for you in Christ Jesus.
1 Timothy 2:1	First of all, then, I ask that supplications, prayers, petitions and thanksgiving be offered for everyone . . .
James 5:16	Therefore, confess your sins to one another and pray for one another, that you may be healed.

Prayer Calendar

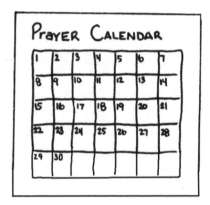

Duplicate and give the students a thirty-day prayer calendar. Don't put the dates with the days so that the calendar can be used month after month. On each day write something or someone they will pray for or how they will pray. This can be the names of those they will pray for, the name of a traditional prayer such as the Our Father, or a type of blessing or devotion that will be prayed.

Drawings or clip art can be used on some of the squares to illustrate an intention.

A prayer calendar can also be used as a source of prayer ideas to help families pray together. The prayer calendar can be posted in a place where the family gathers. The prayer ideas are intergenerational and can be used by any family member. A sample prayer calendar is above.

Our Father Chain

The Our Father is the prayer that Jesus taught his friends. This prayer enables us to put into words what we believe.

Encourage the children to learn to pray the Our Father by making a paper chain. Before class type this prayer in ten separate lines as below. Duplicate a page for each child. Have the children cut apart the lines to form links for the chain. This exercise can be repeated with other traditional prayers.

1. Our Father, who art in heaven,
2. hallowed be thy name;
3. thy kingdom come;
4. thy will be done on earth as it is in heaven.
5. Give us this day our daily bread;
6. and forgive us our trespasses
7. as we forgive those who trespass against us;
8. and lead us not into temptation,
9. but deliver us from evil.
10. Amen.

The challenge for students who are learning the prayer is to put the words together in the correct order. The first link is formed into a circle and secured with tape. The next link is put through the previous one and taped. This process continues until a chain is formed.

Picture Poster

A great teaching tool for the classroom is a prayer poster. Print the word "Pray" in large letters in the middle of a large piece of colored poster board. Select photos from family magazines and mission publications of people who need our prayers. Collect photos from categories like children, families, homeless, missionaries, poor, and sick.

Have the students glue the photos on various colors of construction paper. Then have them glue the construction paper onto the poster board.

This makes an attractive poster for a classroom display. Use the poster as a discussion starter about people who need our prayers. Then ask the children to name other people for whom we should pray.

This is a good way to remind students of their daily call to pray for others.

Morning Prayer

Encourage the children to begin each day with a morning prayer, offering their day to God. The following offering speaks the language of children. It can be prayed in the classroom and at home.

God,
We offer you this day
and everything we do and say.
We ask you to bless us
and bless our families and friends.
Be with us all through the day
as we go about our lives.
Help us to reach out to others
in any way we can.
May all that we do today
give glory to your name.
Amen.

Family Bread

"Family Bread" refers to a special way for families to pray together. As bread is shared, so are blessings with each other.

As a reminder that Jesus is the Bread of Life, give each child a small loaf of bread to take home and share with their families at dinnertime. Small loaves of bread can be purchased at a reasonable price at a bakery thrift shop. Put each loaf in a small re-sealable plastic bag along with the following instructions and prayer.

Family Bread
Place this bread on your family dinner table.
Each person breaks off a piece and gives it with a blessing
to a person seated nearby. Then pray these words:

May this bread remind us of Jesus, the
Bread of Life, who is present in the Eucharist.
May we remember that we are to be bread for others.

Prayer Plant

A prayer plant reminds the children to thank God for the beauty of our world and all creation. It helps them remember that everything God made is good.

Give a small two-inch pot to each student. Plant colorful bedding plants such as begonias in each pot. Duplicate a creation prayer such as the following, and give a copy to each child.

Creation Prayer
Dear God, thank you for plants
and flowers and for all of creation
which you have made for love of us. Amen.

Tell the children to cut out the prayer and glue it to a small twig (like a flag). Then have them carefully push the twig into the dirt around their plant. Tell them to thank God for creation every time they see their prayer plant at home.

Sticker Prayer

Children can make a sticker prayer to give praise to God for the many blessings in their lives. This prayer will help children give thanks to God who is the Creator of all things in our world. It will also remind them to be grateful for what they have.

Make copies of the Praise Prayer on colored paper. Leave room next to each phrase for a colorful sticker.

Let the children select a sticker to illustrate each line. A yellow sun sticker can be used for the first line, gold stick-on stars can illustrate the second line, a people sticker can be used for the third line, and red stick-on hearts can symbolize love in the fourth line. Then the children can glue their praise prayers to a sheet of colored construction paper to form a frame. Encourage the students to display these "sticker" Praise Prayers at home.

Glory Be with Gestures

We are called to life in the Trinity. We live in community as does God who is Father, Son, and Holy Spirit. The traditional Glory Be prayer helps us express our fundamental belief in the Trinity.

This prayer can be taught to the children with gestures. The motions are done by the children to help them understand the meaning of the prayer.

Explain and demonstrate the gestures that symbolize the Trinity prior to praying the prayer. The gesture of outstretched arms for the Father indicates that the Father is with us everywhere. The gesture for the Son symbolizes the nail holes in the hands of Jesus Christ from the crucifixion. For the Holy Spirit we hold our hands over our heart to remind us that the Holy Spirit lives in our hearts and guides us.

Glory Be

Glory be to the Father,
(arms out at sides)
and to the Son,
(point to each palm)
and to the Holy Spirit.
(hands on heart)
As it was in the beginning
(arms out at sides)
Is now and will be forever.
(arms overhead)
Amen.
(hands folded in prayer)

Prayer Rock

We want the children to take what they learned about prayer in the classroom and make it a part of their lives each day. One way to help children remember to say their prayers at night is with a prayer rock.

Collect small rocks or purchase a bag of white landscaping stones. Cut a length of inexpensive fabric into circles eight inches in diameter. Put one rock into each one of the fabric circles. Tie the fabric with a fifteen-inch length of ribbon to keep the rock inside. Duplicate the following rhyme for each child.

Prayer Rock

I'm your little prayer rock
to remind you to pray;
put me on your pillow
all through the day.

Then when night comes
and you climb into bed,
you will see your prayer rock
and say your prayers instead.

Punch a hole in the corner of each verse and put the ribbon through it. Make a prayer rock for each child in this way or, if the children are older, have them make these themselves.

Blessing Ceremony

A blessing ceremony is an appropriate way to end class on occasion. Blessings traditionally call on God to be with us. They are a way of connecting our lives with God.

In a blessing ceremony children come forward and are signed with the sign of the cross on their foreheads. Holy water or blessed oil can be used if desired. Be sure to use each child's name during the blessing. This personalizes the blessing for each child. A simple blessing such as the following may be used. Recite any one of these lines as the child is blessed:

> May you always walk with Jesus.
>
> Live as a child of God.
>
> May the Holy Spirit guide your way.
>
> Walk in the light of Christ.
>
> Live in God's love.
>
> May God bless you in all things.

A blessing helps children experience in a tangible way God's love. Children feel special when they are blessed by a teacher, catechist, or parent.

2
Living in Peace and Justice

Living in peace is not an easy road, yet it is one we are called to follow. Peace is both a collective and an individual effort. To be people of peace, we must learn to look at the common good rather than at individual interests. We must turn away from selfishness and reach out to others in peace and friendship.

Peace and reconciliation begin with us. We take our smaller individual efforts and add them to a larger collective effort to gain peace and hope for all.

Likewise, an essential part of our faith must be a commitment to justice. Justice is the moral virtue that leads people to give their due to God and neighbor. When we work for justice, we help to bring about the kingdom of God. God has given us our world for the good of all people and all nations. God created each of us in God's own image and likeness. Thus each person has the right to be treated with dignity and respect.

Working for both peace and justice involves serving others. This chapter provides opportunities for the students to reach out to others throughout the year.

Walk in Peace Footsteps

We must stress to the children that following Jesus means living in peace with others. This can be a difficult challenge, but it is one that we must take on.

Before class make a "Walk in Peace" form for the students on a half sheet of paper (see below). Title the page "Walk in Peace." At the bottom of the page print "Blessed are the peacemakers" from Matthew 5:9. Duplicate a copy for each child.

Discuss with the children how they can live as peacemakers. Personalize the lesson by inviting the children to pledge to walk in peace. Ask the children to write a way they can live in peace in their lives. Then they should sign their names on the line provided.

The children can take the forms home or bring them forward at a class prayer service as a sign that they will walk in peace with Jesus Christ. This activity helps the children understand that our faith is to be active. The idea of the footprint helps them know that we are not just to learn about our faith, but to actively live it.

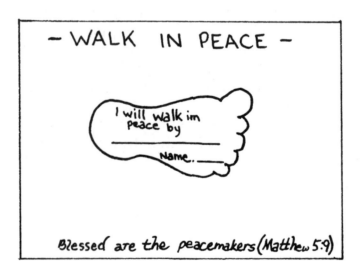

Peace Litany

It is important to pray for peace in our world. One way to do this to have the children pray a litany for peace like the following:

Reader 1:   May there be an end to discrimination and racism.

All: *Lord, help us to live in peace.*

Reader 2:   May we always remember that all people are created in God's image and likeness.

All: *Lord, help us to live in peace.*

Reader 3:   May world leaders put aside differences and work together for the good of all people.

All: *Lord, help us to live in peace.*

Reader 4:   May victims of war and violence find peace in their lives.

All: *Lord, help us to live in peace.*

Reader 5:   May we have the courage to live in peace in our communities, our nation, and our world.

All: *Lord, help us to live in peace.*

Five different children can read the petitions. Everyone else answers with the response.

Peacemaking Actions

The following is a list of a dozen ways children can live in peace with others. Discuss these actions with the children. Ask how they might apply them to their own lives.

- I stuck up for someone when others were making fun of him or her.
- I used words rather than fists when I was angry.
- I shared my things with others.
- I did a favor for someone without expecting a reward.
- I tried to make friends with someone who is different from me.
- I prayed for someone I didn't like.
- I helped someone who was having trouble doing something.
- I used peace words like I'm sorry, I'll help you, and you can go first.
- I forgave someone who had hurt me.
- I let other kids join our game instead of saying they couldn't play.
- I made friends with a person from a different race, culture, or country.
- I found a prayer for peace and asked others to say it too.

With this list as a start, students can be encouraged to think of their own ideas for living in peace. In this way they learn to make peace a part of their lives.

Family Service Day

A Family Service Day is a parish event in which representatives of various social service organizations in the local community are invited to come to the parish hall and set up displays, give short presentations, and offer service projects related to their ministries that families can participate in.

The program begins with a scripture reading. Service activities depend on the needs of a particular community and can include the following:

- assembling care packages for a women's home including sewing kits, soap, lotion, pens, notepads, and similar items.
- filling welcome baskets for those who stay at homeless shelters.
- making place mats for dinner trays at a children's hospital.
- creating silk flowers to be used as corsages for an event at a center for persons who are mentally ill.
- putting together sandwiches for the homeless.
- decorating and assembling gift bags of personal needs items for patients at a rehabilitation center.

Donations of suitable items are solicited from families before this day. At the Family Service Day information is provided for those families who wish to volunteer with a particular organization. This is a wonderful way for children and families to make a difference in their community.

Word Puzzles

The sacrament of reconciliation is an opportunity to think about where we have failed to live as peaceable people. It is a sacrament of healing and forgiveness.

We can help children learn the vocabulary of the sacrament of reconciliation by making two connectable puzzle pieces out of poster board for each vocabulary word and definition below. On one puzzle piece print the word. On the other piece print the short definition. Be sure to vary the size and shape of the puzzle pieces. Here are some possible words and definitions to use for the puzzle pieces

Contrition	*being sorry*
Reconciliation	*making peace*
Confess	*telling your sins to a priest*
Penance	*action or prayer that shows sorrow*
Sacrament	*celebration of God's love*
Sin	*turning away from God*
Absolution	*God forgives me*

Give the children a puzzle piece. Instruct them to find the person holding the piece that matches theirs. Next ask each pair to read the word and definition. Then redistribute the puzzle pieces and repeat the exercise.

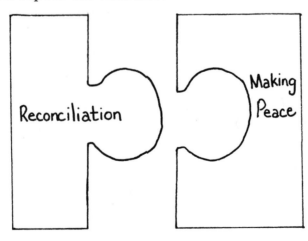

Peace Tree

Jesus tells us "Blessed are the peacemakers, for they shall be called children of God." We are challenged to live as peacemakers.

One way to encourage children to live as people of peace is with a Peace Tree. Set up a potted tree in the hallway or gathering area. Make a sign that proclaims "Our Peace Tree" and place it near the plant. Draw an outline of a dove bearing the word "Peace." Copy the outline onto gold paper for each child.

Spend a few minutes in class with the children talking about living in peace. Some ideas are:

- Forgive someone who has hurt you.
- Say "I'm sorry" when you do something wrong.
- Share with others who have less.
- Be friendly to someone who is new in school.
- Listen carefully to what others have to say.
- Pray for the needs of other people.

Have the children cut out one of the peace doves. Tell them to write on the back of the dove one thing they will do for peace. Punch a hole in the top of the dove. Take a piece of gold yarn and hang the dove on the Peace Tree.

The tree is a reminder to live in peace in the name of Jesus Christ. It is a source of learning for the students who create the Peace Tree as well as all those who see it.

Class Poster

Children need visual reminders in order to remind them to make justice a part of their lives. Working together to create a class poster helps students to remember our common call to work for justice.

In the center of a large piece of poster board print the words "Work for Justice." Next, ask each student to draw around one hand on a sheet of colored construction paper. Provide a variety of colors such as blue, orange, yellow, red, brown, purple, and green. Then each student should write his or her name inside the hand shape. Finally, have the students cut out the hand shapes and glue them to the poster board.

Emphasize to the children that we can use our hands to reach out to others. We must use our talents and abilities to promote the cause of justice. We must offer a helping hand to people in need.

This makes a colorful class poster that personalizes the lesson for the students and help them realize that they are to live what they are learning. Display the poster on the classroom bulletin board as a reminder that all of us must work for justice.

Awareness Activity

The art contest described below can help students realize that there is an unequal distribution of the world's resources. This activity is a concrete way of showing children why it is important to live in justice.

Give out butterfly patterns. Tell the students that there is an art contest for the most colorful and creative butterfly. Then give out envelopes of crayons. Before class mark the envelopes with a 1, 2, 3, or 4. In the number 1 envelopes put eight crayons, in the number 2 envelopes put three crayons, in the number 3 envelopes put two crayons, and in the number 4 envelopes put one crayon.

Ask the students with the same number on their envelopes to sit together. Direct the students to color the butterfly as creatively as possible using only the crayons in their envelopes. Choose five of the most colorful butterflies and post them on the bulletin board.

Then discuss this activity with the children. Ask the children who had only one, two, or three crayons to explain how they felt during the contest. Ask the children who had all eight crayons to explain how they felt when they saw that they had more crayons than the others. Discuss who had the best chance of winning the contest and why. Discuss who had the least chance of winning the contest and why. Ask how they felt about this art contest. Ask the students what they think Jesus would do in a contest like this. Then ask the students to think of ways to respond to the needs of those who have less than we do.

Justice Cards

One way to help children see how they can put their faith into action is with justice cards. Justice cards can be made as follows.

Type the following situations as below. Cut the typed sheets apart to make individual cards.

- One student makes jokes about people of another culture. Everyone laughs. *What can you do?*

- Your aunt gave you $10 for your birthday. She said to spend it any way you want. *What can you do with the money?*

- You see a new student looking for a place to sit. This child is of a different race than you. *What can you do to make that person feel welcome?*

- Your church announces a canned food drive. People are to bring non-perishable foods to Mass next week. *What are ways you can help?*

- A refugee family has just moved into your neighborhood. They fled from a war-torn country. *What can you do for this family?*

Gather the students into a circle. Place the cards face down in the middle of each group. Ask for a volunteer to read the top card. Then have the students discuss the situation described with their group. Have the students repeat the process for the other cards.

> **JUSTICE CARD**
>
> One student makes jokes about people of another culture. Everyone laughs.
>
> *What can you do?*

Creative thinkers are needed in our world. We must encourage creative ideas for situations in our lives and in our world as we work for justice for all people. This type of discussion helps to do that.

Justice Checklist

Social justice is an important part of our faith. Catholic social teaching and a commitment to the poor must be shared at all levels of faith formation.

Give a copy of the Justice Checklist (below) to each student. Ask the students to individually check off the items that apply to them. Then discuss each item with the students in class. They do not need to reveal which items they checked.

Justice Checklist

Check the items on this page that apply to you.

_____ I help others when I see a need.

_____ I pray for the needs of other people.

_____ I volunteer my time for the good of other people.

_____ I treat other people with respect.

_____ I contribute part of my money to help the hungry.

_____ I speak up when I see an injustice.

_____ I use less so others will have more.

_____ I bring canned food for the parish food pantry.

_____ I donate items I don't need to others.

_____ I encourage others to get involved.

Encourage the students to take home the checklist as a reminder to act justly each and every day.

Forgiveness Chain

It is often difficult for children to ask forgiveness of others in their lives or to grant forgiveness to someone who has hurt them because they don't know what words to listen for or to say. Discuss with the children what words they can use to ask or give forgiveness. Phrases like the following can be useful to children:

I'm sorry.
Please forgive me.
I forgive you.
Peace be with you.
You're forgiven.
I was wrong.

To help the children remember these words and phrases, show them how to make forgiveness chains. On individual paper strips ask the children to write a forgiveness phrase and decorate the strip. Repeat the process with other phrases and strips. Then have the children tape their links together.

The completed chain is a reminder that we are to ask forgiveness of people we have injured by our words or our actions. We must also forgive those who have hurt us. Link all the forgiveness chains together for display in the classroom.

Making Choices

To encourage the children to live in peace, discuss situations in which they have to decide how to act. This is a practical idea that helps students understand that they do have choices in life. We stress to the students that we cannot control what happens to us, but we always have a choice about how we respond.

Following are some scenarios that can be discussed in class to help children learn that they are to live as reconciling people:

- You spill a drink on your sister's art project for school. She worked really hard on it. What can you do?
- One of the students in your class says mean things to another student. You overhear this in the hallway. Should you do something?
- You receive too much change when you buy something in a store. The clerk doesn't notice. What should you do?
- A classmate pushes you out of the way and others laugh. This makes you angry. How should you act?
- You yell at your younger brother for bothering you. He just wanted you to read a story to him. How can you make it up to him?
- You see one student shove another student in the hall. The student isn't hurt. Is this your business?
- You are angry because you have been treated unfairly. You know it wasn't your fault. What are your choices?

Stress that there are other situations that will come up. Remind the children that as followers of Jesus Christ we are to live as peacemakers in our lives. We are to choose peace.

Pledge of Nonviolence

Encourage the children to make a pledge of nonviolence with their families. This is a concrete method of doing something about the violence in our world.

In the family pledge of nonviolence, encourage all family members to

- respect self and others.
- communicate better.
- listen to one another.
- forgive.
- respect nature.
- enjoy one another's company.
- challenge violence in all forms.

A pledge of nonviolence asks families to learn to listen and forgive. It helps us become nonviolent and peaceable people in a world filled with violence. It is a tool to help people take positive steps to challenge violence at school, work, and in the community.

A family pledge of nonviolence helps families take a stand for peace in our world today. It helps us become more peaceable people. Together we can make a difference.

A sample pledge is available from the Institute for Peace and Justice, 4144 Lindell Blvd. #408, St. Louis, MO 63108 or at several websites that promote peace and justice.

Prayer for Justice

We are called to help bring about the kingdom of God. Ask the children to pray for justice in our world. Pray the following "Prayer for Justice."

Prayer for Justice

Father of us all, we praise you
as the Creator of all things
and all people.

Teach us to be the people
you desire us to be.
Help us to see the face of your Son, Jesus,
in every person.

Send us your Spirit
that we may walk in peace
and live in justice.

Amen.

Continue to stress to the children the importance of prayer. Remind the children of the necessity of working for justice in our world and that with God all things are possible.

3
Exploring the Bible

The Bible is the book of the church and the story of our faith. The Bible details God's unfailing love for all people.

We must help the children understand that the Bible is God's word. We must also help the children learn that the Bible contains many different books and types of literature by many different authors.

The Old Testament shows how the Israelites struggled to be faithful to God. It tells of God's promise to them to be their God.

In the New Testament, the gospels tell of the saving actions of Jesus. The gospels developed in three stages. First was the life, death, and resurrection of Jesus. Next, the stories were shared by the apostles with others. Then the stories were written down and collected. The Acts of the Apostles and the letters and epistles show how the early Christians tried to live the teachings of Jesus. As they faced new situations, they struggled to live their faith each day.

The Bible has been passed on from generation to generation in the church and interpreted within the church. With the help of the Holy Spirit the message of God's word lives on in the lives of all Christians today.

Bible Tour

This lesson helps children to become familiar with the entire Bible. Necessary for this lesson is a bible of the same version for each child.

Explain to the children that the Bible is the word of God. Have them turn to the page between the Old and New Testaments. Tell them that the Bible is divided into two main parts. Ask if anyone can name the first part of the Bible. Then direct the children to turn to the first page of the Old Testament. Ask someone to give that page number. (Using page numbers helps involve those students who are not at all familiar with the Bible.) Explain that the Old Testament tells the story of God and the people of Israel prior to the birth of Jesus.

Then ask if anyone can name the second part of the Bible. Direct the children to turn to the first page of the New Testament. Ask someone to give that page number. The New Testament—especially the gospels—tells the story of the life, death, and resurrection of Jesus.

Tell the children that both the Old and New Testaments are further divided into books. Ask for a volunteer to name the first book of the Old Testament (Genesis). Tell everyone to turn to the first page of Genesis. Ask someone to give that page number. Explain that the first story in Genesis is the story of how God created the world.

Call on another student to name the first book of the New Testament (Matthew) and its page number. Do the same with the other three gospels. Explain that the gospels are about the life of Jesus. Show how each book is divided into chapter and verse. Give an example such as Matthew 6:9 and have the children locate it. When they do, call on a volunteer to read the passage aloud.

Ask the students to locate the Acts of the Apostles. Let someone give the page number on which it begins. Explain that this book and those that follow are the story of how the early Christians followed Jesus Christ and how the church began. Read a sampling from Acts 1–3.

This lesson helps beginning Bible students learn, while giving experienced Bible users a chance to participate.

Creation Pantomime

The beautiful Bible story of creation in Genesis 1:1-31 tells us how God made everything in the world and how people were made in God's own image. This story also stresses that everything God made is good. A way to help the children remember this story is with an echo pantomime. The children echo the words and actions of the teacher line by line as follows.

In the beginning God created
the heavens and the earth.

(cross arms at wrist and raise slowly,
then uncross up high)

Then God said "Let there be plants
and trees."

(place hands near the floor
and then high above head)

And God said, "Let there be a sun
and a moon and stars."

(form a round sun with the fingers,
then wiggle fingers for stars)

Then God made the fish in the water
and the birds in the sky.

(move one hand like fish swimming,
then hook thumbs and wave hands)

God made the animals, big
and little.

(stretch arms far apart,
then move hands close together)

Then God made people in
his own image.

(open arms, then place hands
on heart)

And God saw that everything
he made was good.

(nod head, then open arms wide)

The actions of an echo pantomime help the children understand and remember the story of creation from the Bible and the lesson that everything God made is good.

Psalm in Parts

Psalms have been used to praise God for thousands of years. Have the children pray Psalm 67 in two parts, a left side and a right side of the classroom. Psalm 67 calls on all the nations of the world to praise the Lord. Pray the psalm in parts as follows:

Psalm 67

Left: May God be gracious to us and bless us;
may God's face shine upon us.

Right: So shall your rule be known upon the earth,
your saving power among all the nations.

Left: May the peoples praise you, God; may all the peoples praise you!

Right: May the nations be glad and shout for joy;
for you govern the peoples justly, you guide the nations upon the earth.

Left: May the peoples praise you, God; may all the peoples praise you!

Right: The earth has yielded its harvest; God, our God, blesses us.

Left: May God bless us still, that the ends of the earth may revere our God.

Bible Verse Guess

This is a game designed to help the students review gospel verses. Some of the gospel verses that can be used to play this game are:

Make disciples of all nations	Matthew 28:19
Blessed are the peacemakers	Matthew 5:9
Let the children come to me	Mark 10:14
Love the Lord your God	Mark 12:30
This is my body	Luke 22:19
Love your enemies	Luke 6:27
I am the light of the world	John 8:12
In the beginning was the Word	John 1:1

To play this game make a dash on the chalkboard for each letter in the first Bible verse. Leave space between the words in the verse. Divide the class into two teams. Call on a student from Team 1 to guess a letter. If a student guesses correctly, print that letter in the correct place. Then the team can confer and get one guess at saying what the entire verse might be. If the letter guess or verse guess is incorrect, a student on Team 2 gets a turn until finally the verse is correctly guessed.

Continue on in the same fashion with other verses.

Book Basket

Many Bible stories have been retold in brightly illustrated books just for children. Provide such a collection of illustrated Bible story books for young children to browse during Mass. Be sure to get the pastor's permission for this project.

Place the books in a large basket. Attach a note to the basket with the following instruction and explanation:

The books in this basket

are for young children

to look at quietly during Mass.

Please return the book you borrow

to the basket after Mass.

Preschoolers will enjoy looking at a Bible book during Mass. In this way they will become familiar with gospel stories in a way they can understand.

Salt of the Earth Project

Jesus often used parables to help his followers understand the meaning of God's kingdom. In Matthew 5:13 Jesus calls us to be salt of the earth. This example of salt reminds us that we are to witness to the teachings of Jesus Christ in our lives. As salt diffuses throughout the food, so we are to go out into the world to spread the teachings of Christ.

As a reminder of this gospel make little bags of rock salt to give to each child. Before class make tags that say:

You are salt of the earth.

Make a difference today.

Place approximately two tablespoons of rock salt (the kind for making ice cream) in an eight inch square of white fabric. Gather the edges and tie with a fifteen-inch length of purple yarn. The edges of the fabric can be fringed if desired. Punch a hole in the tag and tie it on using the yarn.

Place all the bags of salt in a basket. At the end of class—after reading and discussing Matthew 5:13—invite each child to take home one of the bags. In this way the children are reminded to be salt of the earth and witness to Christ in the world.

Meditation on Loaves and Fishes

Scripture helps the children to reflect on how God's word can be lived in their lives. The following meditation is based on the story of the loaves and fishes from Matthew 14:13-21. First, read the story from the Bible. Then, ask the children to sit quietly, close their eyes, and listen carefully. Say:

> Imagine yourself in the gospel story of the loaves and fishes that we heard today. You are on the hillside with Jesus. The sun is warm on your back. The ground is hard as you sit and listen to Jesus teach the people. You share the surprising meal of bread and fish with the others.
>
> When the people finally begin to go home, you stay behind. As the apostles are busy gathering up the leftovers, you walk up to where Jesus is standing.
>
> Jesus sees you coming and smiles. You talk to him about what happened. You say, "Jesus, you shared food with us today when we were hungry. You shared your words with us too. I know that you want us to share with others." Jesus nods.
>
> Then you ask, "But how can I do that in my life? I already have so much to do."
>
> What answer does Jesus give to you?

Do not ask the children to share their thoughts. This is a personal reflection and an opportunity for the children to know that God speaks to them through scripture.

What Does God Ask of Us?

The gospels are filled with accounts of how Jesus forgave people and called on them to forgive others. Choose one of the following gospel stories. Read it together with the class. Discuss what these words of Jesus tell us about forgiveness.

Forgiving father	Luke 15:11-32
Lost sheep	Luke 15:1-7
Zacchaeus	Luke 19:1-10
Lost coin	Luke 15:8-10
Forgive and you will be forgiven	Luke 6:37
Apostles can forgive sins	John 20:19-23
Be reconciled with one another	Matthew 5:23-24
Blessed are the merciful	Matthew 5:7
Forgive our trespasses	Matthew 6:12
Forgive seventy-seven times	Matthew 18:21-22

Another variation of the lesson is to divide the students into small groups (three to four students each) and assign each group a different story. They discuss the story in their small groups. Then call on one student in each group to summarize the discussion for the whole class.

Jesus Pledge

God's word speaks to our lives. Mark 1:16-20 recounts the story of Jesus' calling of his first followers. Peter, Andrew, James, and John were fishermen who left everything behind to follow Jesus. This gospel reading calls us to be followers of Jesus also. Explain to the students that the fish is a symbol of Christianity.

Read the Bible story to the students. Then ask the students to make a pledge to follow Jesus Christ. Use the following format for a Jesus Pledge.

On a half sheet of white paper make the outline of a large fish. Inside the fish print "I will follow Jesus Christ." Add a line for the students to sign their names. Duplicate these pages on many different colors of paper for each student.

Ask the students to cut out the fish, read the pledge, and sign it. Have the children place their signed Jesus Pledges in a basket on the class prayer table. The Jesus Pledge can serve as a reminder to always follow Jesus.

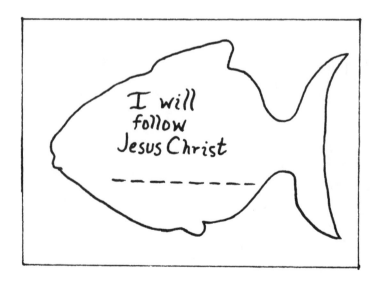

Blind Man Play

Jesus performed many miracles. The story of the cure of the blind man in Mark 10:46-52 shows us that Jesus calls all people to follow him on his journey. Have the children act out the gospel story in play form. Choose one student to be Jesus, the other to be Bartimaeus. The rest of the students can play the "crowd" seated on left and right sides of the room.

Make a copy of the script for students in the crowd. The Jesus and Bartimaeus characters should memorize their parts. The stage area can be the front of the classroom.

The Story of the Blind Man

Jesus: (*walking across the stage from the left with two others*) Let's go. Its time to leave Jericho.

Bartimaeus: (*sitting on the floor*) Jesus, I'm blind. Have pity on me.

Side 1: Be quiet, stop that noise.

Side 2: Jesus doesn't have time for you.

Bartimaeus: Jesus, I'm blind. Have pity on me.

Jesus: (*stopping*) Call him over here.

Side 1: Get up, Jesus wants to see you. Hurry.

Side 2: (*pointing to Bartimaeus*) Here, Jesus, this is the man who was calling to you.

Jesus: What do you want me to do for you?

Bartimaeus: Jesus, I want to see.

Jesus: Go your way, your faith has saved you.

Bartimaeus: (*getting up, moving around*) I can see! I can see! Jesus, I will follow you always.

Scripture Story Questions

Class discussion helps children to come to a better understanding of the Bible. Use the following discussion questions after reading the students the story of Jesus calming the sea from Luke 8:22-25.

The story tells how Jesus and his disciples were in a boat on the lake. While Jesus was asleep, a storm came up. The apostles were afraid and woke up Jesus. He calmed the storm and then said to the disciples, "Where is your faith?"

Discussion Questions

Where were the disciples and Jesus?

What happened on the lake?

Why did the disciples wake up Jesus?

What did Jesus do?

What did Jesus say to the disciples?

How could Jesus calm a storm?

When were times when you have been afraid?

What do you do when you are afraid?

How do you trust Jesus?

How is Jesus with us today?

Discussion helps the children remember the Bible story and see how the story can be applied to their own lives.

Thanking God

In the Bible story in Luke 17:11-19 Jesus heals ten lepers. However, only one leper comes back to thank him. Jesus asks the one, "Where are the other nine?" This is the leper we are to imitate. We are to remember to give thanks and praise to our God.

After discussing this story encourage the class to write a thank-you litany to God in the format described below. Read things that the students are grateful for, with the children responding "Thank you, God" after each phrase.

Reader: For the sun and stars,
Children: Thank you, God.

Reader: For food,
Children: Thank you, God.

Reader: For animals,
Children: Thank you, God.

Reader: For lakes, mountains, and trees,
Children: Thank you, God.

Reader: For family and friends,
Children: Thank you, God.

Reader: For all of us here,
Children: Thank you, God.

Share with Others

Jesus teaches us that we are to share with others without counting the cost.

The story of the rich young man in Matthew 19:16-22 represents that lesson well. The rich young man comes to Jesus and asks him what good he must do to gain eternal life. Jesus tells him to sell his possessions and give everything to the poor. Only then can he follow Jesus. But the young man goes away sad because he does not want to give up what he has.

Read the story to the students from the Bible. Check for a sense of understanding. Questions help the children learn what the story means in their lives. Ask discussion questions such as the following to check their knowledge.

What did the rich young man ask Jesus?
What did Jesus tell him?
What did the young man do?
What do you find difficult about giving to others?
Why do you think Jesus wants us to help the poor?
How can we share with others?

This gospel story challenges us to live a life of service to others. We are to share the world's resources so that all people have what they need.

Good Shepherd Cross

The story of the Good Shepherd is found in John 10:11-16. This portrayal of Jesus as Good Shepherd helps us understand that Jesus cares about each one of us. When we stray, Jesus looks for us and welcomes us home. He protects us and gives his life for us.

To remind the children of this image of Jesus as Good Shepherd, have the children make Good Shepherd crosses. Instruct the children to cut out paper crosses, seven inches by nine inches from brown construction paper and circles—three inches in diameter— from yellow construction paper, or prepare the materials beforehand. Glue a yellow circle to the center of the cross. Finally, provide a sticker of Jesus the Good Shepherd to be placed in the center of the circle.

The Good Shepherd crosses can then be laminated for durability if desired. They can be pinned to a bulletin board, taped to a wall, or taken home. The cross is a reminder for all to follow Jesus the Good Shepherd.

4
Welcoming Advent and Christmas

The season of Advent is a time of expectation, waiting, caring, compassion, kindness, and hope. We celebrate that the promise to the people of God is fulfilled. Besides remembering the first Christmas, Advent is also a season to remember that Jesus will come again at the end of time. The Christmas season is a time to live in peace, and to remember that Jesus came for all cultures, all nations, and all people.

During the four weeks of Advent we prepare our hearts and our lives so that we will be able to fully celebrate Christmas. We must encourage the children to live Advent as a season distinct from Christmas. Children need to hear the message that the month of December is about more than shopping and parties.

The seasons of Advent and Christmas should be a time of reconciliation and forgiveness, a time of reaching out to those we may have hurt by our words and our actions. They are seasons in which we reflect on and continue our journey with Jesus.

Yes, Advent and Christmas are seasons to put the commercial pursuits on the back burner. Instead we must keep the light of Christ before us. The lessons and activities in this chapter encourage the children to respond in this way.

Four Weeks of Advent

Ask the students to make a different prayer intention for each week of Advent and to follow up on the intentions by doing related activities. Pray for that intention in class and also encourage the children to pray at home. In this way the children will learn that Advent is a time of prayer and a time of reaching out to others. Examples of four weeks of prayer intentions and related activities follow.

Week 1

Prayer Intention: Pray for the sick.

Background: We are called to follow Jesus in showing care for all people. There are many occasions in the gospels where Jesus cares for the sick. We are to help others and to pray for them. All of us are part of God's family.

Activities: Collect items for a children's hospital. Watch a video about the life of Mother Teresa. Make get well cards for someone who is sick. Read and discuss the story of the Good Samaritan in Luke 10:29-37.

Week 2

Prayer intention: Pray for the hungry.

Background: There are many people in our world who go to bed hungry due to conditions in the country where they live. We must reach out a helping hand to others. We must see the face of Jesus in all people.

Activities: Conserve resources. Donate food to the parish food pantry. Contribute to Catholic Relief Services. Read and discuss the works of mercy in Matthew 25:35-40.

Week 3

Prayer intention: Pray for forgiveness and reconciliation.

Background: Ours is a merciful and loving God who always forgives us. We must make up for any harm we have caused. We are also called to forgive others in our lives. In this way we follow Jesus who shared God's forgiveness with other people.

Activities: Let go of grudges. Say the Our Father. Participate in the sacrament of reconciliation. Read and discuss the story of the lost sheep in Luke 15:1-7.

Week 4

Prayer intention: Pray for world peace.

Background: We are called to live in peace. Jesus, the Prince of Peace, demands that we look for peaceful resolutions to our conflicts.

Activities: Stand up for someone who is treated unfairly. Pray the Prayer of St. Francis. Refuse to listen to jokes that demean people. Read the story of loving our enemies in Matthew 5:43-48.

Advent Story

Children enjoy hearing stories. This helps them learn the lesson in an interesting way. Read the following story from *Kid Collection Lectionary-Based Resources: Cycle B* as a reminder of what the season is all about. A second option is to divide the story in parts and have the children do the reading in play form, with one person playing Rachel, one person playing Jerome, and a third playing the narrator.

"What are you doing, Jerome?" Rachel asked.

Jerome was sitting on the floor. Scattered around him were papers and boxes, tangled strings of lights and bright tinsel garland. "It's the first day of Advent. It's time to get ready for Christmas."

Rachel shook her head. "I haven't even thought about it yet," she sighed.

"Well, you better start," Jerome admitted. "Advent is the time to buy presents, send out Christmas cards, and make a list of what you want."

Rachel was silent for a while; then she spoke softly. "I don't know, Jerome. Father said at Mass that Advent isn't just about decorating and shopping and baking and making out lists of things for people to give us. He said that's not what Jesus wants."

"Probably not," Jerome said. "But that's what everybody does during Advent. We can't change the world, can we?" The two friends sat in silence, each one thinking their own thoughts.

"No," Rachel finally agreed, "we can't change the world, but we can change ourselves. Jesus said, 'Stay awake and watch carefully.' He wants us ready when he comes again."

"What do you mean, comes again?" Jerome wondered. "Like another Christmas?"

"Nobody knows," Rachel said. "But Jesus says we have to be ready."

"But how?" Jerome asked.

"Well, we can do all the same things as getting ready for Christmas, but do them for Jesus."

"You mean like instead of making a Christmas list, we'll make a list of things we can do for Jesus?" Jerome asked.

"And for others," Rachel said. "Remember, Jesus said that whatever we do for others, we also do for him."

Jerome's mind started racing with ideas. "We can make our morning prayer a getting ready prayer and ask Jesus to fill us with his love."

"That's good!" Rachel agreed. "And we can use our allowances to buy presents for poor children. We can collect canned goods for the basket at church. We can make cards for people in the nursing home. And get some other kids together to sing carols for children in the hospital."

As Rachel and Jerome talked, the light of God's love in their hearts kept getting brighter and brighter. They were getting ready for Jesus. Are you ready for Jesus?

Seasonal Meditation

The following Advent meditation prayer is for classroom use. Choose five children to read the various parts. The rest of the class responds as indicated.

Child 1:   Advent is a season of hope.
               Every time we help a person in need,
               we live the season of Advent.
All: Come, Lord Jesus, into our hearts and our lives.
               Teach us to walk in your way.

Child 2:   Advent is a season of peace.
               Every time we forgive someone who has hurt us,
               we live the season of Advent.
All: Come, Lord Jesus, into our hearts and our lives.
               Teach us to walk in your way.

Child 3:   Advent is a season of light.
               Every time we make a new person feel welcome,
               we live the season of Advent.
All: Come, Lord Jesus, into our hearts and our lives.
               Teach us to walk in your way.

Child 4:   Advent is a season of love.
               Every time we speak in love and not in anger,
               we live the season of Advent.
All: Come, Lord Jesus, into our hearts and our lives.
               Teach us to walk in your way.

Child 5:   Advent is a season to share.
               Every time we reach out and help others,
               we live the season of Advent.
All: Come, Lord Jesus, into our hearts and our lives.
               Teach us to walk in your way.

This prayer encourages the children to pray to Jesus that their hearts will be made ready for Christmas.

Family Packet

A Family Packet is designed to help families keep the season of Advent in their hearts and minds.

A Family Packet can be made by duplicating a series of Advent ideas on individual pieces of paper topped with a cover sheet with the words "Family Packet" and a drawing of an Advent wreath or other Advent symbol. Also include the name of your church or school.

Provide a variety of activities in the Family Packet. Be sure to include only those ideas for which copyright permission is given with the material or secured from the publisher. A Family Packet for Advent might include:

- an explanatory letter.
- a calendar with something to do each day of Advent.
- Advent wreath prayers.
- discussion questions on the Sunday readings during Advent.
- the story of St. Nicholas.
- an activity sheet to fill in for each week of Advent.
- an Advent family prayer.
- information on a parish service project during this season.
- a list of parish events during Advent.

Send home the Family Packets with your students or distribute them after Sunday Mass.

Advent Prayer Chain

A paper chain with written Advent prayers is a helpful and prayerful way for the children to mark the days until Christmas. Duplicate the prayers below for each day of the Advent season.

Put the following prayers on the prayer chain, one per link. Type half of the prayers on one sheet, leaving room for them to be cut apart. Duplicate them on purple paper. Type the other half on a separate sheet, then duplicate on white paper. Have the students cut out the links and form a chain, with the words of the prayer facing in.

Tell the children to take off a loop each day and say the prayer inside.

When all the links are opened and all the prayers are said, it will be Christmas!

Prayers

1. Jesus, help us to care about others during Advent.
2. Holy Spirit, fill our hearts with love for others.
3. Father, help us to remember that you love us with an unending love.
4. God, help us to get ready in our hearts to celebrate Christmas.
5. Lord, may we be a joyful people during Advent and always.
6. Jesus, teach us to help others as did St. Nicholas.
7. Spirit of God, be with us in all that we do.
8. Dear Lord, help us to live as people of your light.
9. God, help us to open our hearts and our lives to people in need.
10. Father, we pray today for all those who are hungry in our world.
11. Jesus, we offer you everything we do today.
12. Lord, forgive us for the times we have hurt you and others.
13. Father, help us have faith in your goodness and love.
14. Lord, help us to live as people of hope.
15. God, help us to say yes in our lives as Mary did in hers.
16. Lord Jesus, may we see you in all the people we meet.
17. Father, help us to share your love with others.
18. Jesus, help us to live in faith, hope, and love through the year.
19. Father, may we see Advent as a time of new beginning.
20. Jesus, help us to stand up for the rights of others.
21. Father, we pray for all those who are sick.
22. Lord, help us to live in peace with one another.
23. God, may we give glory to you by the way we live our lives.
24. Father, thank you for the gift of Christmas.

Advent Poster

This activity calls for the students to make individual Advent posters in class. The completed posters can be displayed in the classroom or the hallway of the school or parish.

Make the posters on 8 1/2" by 11" paper. Use a computer or hand letter each poster. Print "Advent is . . ." on the top. At the bottom, put a word that represents a dimension of the season. Several children may have the same wording. For example:

- Advent is . . . caring
- Advent is . . . hope
- Advent is . . . sharing
- Advent is . . . love
- Advent is . . . helping
- Advent is . . . giving

Ask the children to illustrate their Advent posters with a drawing or symbol. This activity helps the students personalize the lessons of Advent.

Giving Tree

A Giving Tree is a Christmas tree with gift requests for needy children or organizations printed on paper ornaments. The tree should be set up in the church vestibule, parish hall, or school hallway during Advent. Put a sign underneath the tree that says "Giving Tree."

On the back of each paper ornament put an item needed by a sponsoring organization (e.g., dish towels, jackets, food supplies) or by children (e.g., gift for a twelve-year-old girl, toy for a five-year-old boy). Punch a hole in the top of each ornament and put gold cord through it. Make a loop with a bow at the top. Hang the ornaments on the tree.

Publicize the Giving Tree at Mass and around the parish. Families take a paper ornament from the tree during Advent and purchase the item listed. The items are gift wrapped (in the case of toys) and placed underneath the tree by a specific date. The ornament should be taped to the top of the gift as a designation of what it is inside. This will help with sorting and delivery, which should be done well before Christmas.

An idea related to the Giving Tree is a Book Tree. A Book Tree is likewise a Christmas tree set up in a common area. Children bring in new books for children of all ages and place them on the tree as ornaments or under the tree when the tree is full. The books are donated to any service agency in need of new books, for example after school programs, subsidized day care programs, and homeless shelters.

Prayer for Advent

Advent is a season of prayer. The following prayer can be used with a group of children. Divide the class into three groups. Make a copy of the prayer for each child. Have each group read aloud their designated part.

Group 1: God, you are the Father
and Creator of us all.
You fulfilled your promise
to your people
and sent us a Savior.
We give you glory and praise.

Group 2: God, you are Jesus Christ,
our hope and our salvation.
As we journey
through this holy Advent season,
help us to have faith in you,
hope for the future,
and love for all people.

Group 3: God, you are the Holy Spirit.
Hear our prayers
and guide us.
May we live always
as people of the light.

All: Amen.

Hand Shaped Ornaments

Children can learn about Advent as a season of caring by creating a hand shaped ornament.

Provide construction paper in colors such as red, green, yellow, and blue. Ask the children to use a pencil and draw around one of their hands. Then explain that they will have the opportunity to decorate a Christmas tree with their hand shapes as a reminder to care about others. If several grade levels are doing this project, each grade can use a different color so that the children can see what they can accomplish when several groups work together.

Next, have the children carefully cut out their hand shapes and print their names with a marker. Have the children punch a hole in the palm of the hand and insert a fifteen-inch piece of yarn (same color as the paper) as a hanger.

Discuss with the children ways they can make a positive difference during Advent. Older children may wish to write some of these ways on the fingers of the ornament. For example:

- helping a brother or sister
- saying a prayer for people in need
- donating food to the food pantry
- buying a toy for a collection
- making a Christmas card for a lonely neighbor
- being polite to someone they do not like.

Allow the students to hang their hand shaped ornaments on a Christmas tree at the school or parish. The hand shaped ornaments will be a reminder to who all who see them that we are to reach out to others during the season of Advent and beyond.

Story of the Manger

Share the wonderful story of the first Christmas manger scene, called a crèche.

St. Francis of Assisi wanted people to remember the true meaning of Christmas. He felt that people were too concerned about parties, decorations, and clothing, and not as concerned with remembering God's great love for us. He asked a friend to help him prepare something special for Christmas in a cave near the town of Greccio, Italy.

A woman in the town was to act as Mary and a man was asked to be Joseph. A manger was prepared and filled with hay. And a baby was to be laid in the manger to represent the Christ Child. Local people agreed to be shepherds. Animals were brought into the cave. The scene at Bethlehem was recreated.

On Christmas Eve people came to the cave. They were amazed when they saw the manger scene with the people, the baby, and the animals. They remembered that Christmas was about the Christ Child born in Bethlehem. In this way Francis touched the hearts of the people.

Show a crèche scene to the students. Tell them that looking at the baby in the manger should remind us to turn our hearts and our thoughts toward Jesus Christ, born for us in Bethlehem as the light of the world.

Christmas Promise

Christmas is more than one day. It is a season that extends well past December 25 to the feast of the Baptism of the Lord.

Talk with the children about ways they can live the spirit of the Christmas season, such as contributing to a food collection, helping an elderly neighbor, saying a prayer for peace, giving their allowance to a children's charity, and reaching out to a lonely child. Ask the students to contribute other ideas.

One way to help children remember to reach out to others is with a Christmas promise. Make a form such as the one below on a half sheet of paper. Add your own clip art or provide Christmas stickers for the children to add.

Duplicate a Christmas promise for each child. Using green paper or printing with green ink on white paper, have the children write what they will do to live the true meaning of the Christmas season. They should also sign their names. Stress the importance of living up to their Christmas promise. Tell them to take the completed form home as a reminder.

CHRISTMAS PROMISE

During this Christmas Season

I will _ _ _ _ _ _ _ _

to make the world a better place.

NAME _ _ _ _ _ _ _

Prayer for Christmas

At Christmastime we pray to show our gratitude to God and to ask for God's help in all we do. Make copies of the following prayer for the students to pray throughout the season in the classroom and at home.

Father, we thank you
for the gift of your Son,
Jesus Christ.

May we share the good news
as did the angels in Bethlehem
on the first Christmas.

Guide us to live the spirit of Christmas
throughout the year
and throughout our lives.

We ask this through
the help of the Holy Spirit,
through whom all things are possible.

Amen.

Wreath of Stars

The story of the Epiphany in Matthew 2:1-12 tells how the wise men followed a star to find Jesus. They did not give up until they found Jesus. Because of this story the star is a popular decoration for Epiphany. Children can make a wreath of stars as a reminder of the lesson that Jesus came for all nations and all people.

Have the children cut out fifteen-inch diameter rings from green poster board and four-inch diameter stars from green, red, and yellow construction paper. (It is suggested that you give a star pattern to each student.) Each student needs to make four stars of each color for a total of twelve stars.

The stars should be glued to the wreath using a glue stick, alternating the colors for the most dynamic look possible. This bright wreath of stars can be hung up at home on an interior door as a reminder of Epiphany.

Star of Jesus

Another Epiphany idea is for the children to sign their names to individual stars of Jesus. This will be a reminder for them to follow the star leading to Jesus.

Before class duplicate and cut out a star for each child on gold paper with the words "I will follow the star of Jesus" printed inside. A signature line should also be included.

During class, read the Epiphany story from Matthew 2:1-12. Then give each child a star and ask them to sign it as a promise to live this pledge in their lives. Then ask the children to cut out their individual stars.

The individual stars can be used in many ways. They can be taken home as a reminder to the students to follow Jesus. They can be offered as part of a class prayer service or Mass. The stars can be placed in a basket on the class prayer table. They can also be used as bulletin board decorations.

5
Walking Through Lent and Easter

Lent is a time of conversion, a time to turn our hearts and our lives toward the light of Christ. Lent's forty days prepare us for Easter.

Living Lent is a challenge and an opportunity to confront those things that keep us away from an awareness of God's presence in our own lives and in the people around us. This is a time to change our hearts and try to become all that God created us to be.

Lent leads us to Holy Week and the Triduum where we celebrate in a special way the life, death, and resurrection of Jesus Christ. The special observances and liturgies of this week speak to the heart of our faith and what we believe. The Easter season that follows helps us focus on the new life that Jesus brings us through his resurrection. It is a time to rejoice in the hope of Jesus Christ. Easter is not the end of Lent, but the beginning of new life for all people.

Remind the students that Easter is not a one day holiday, but a fifty day celebration. For this reason, this chapter provides lessons and activities for the duration of the Easter season leading to a joyful celebration of Pentecost.

Prayer for Lent

Ash Wednesday is the beginning of Lent. Near this day, encourage the children to pray together the following prayer. Duplicate copies for each student.

Jesus, as we begin this holy season of Lent,
we ask you to be with us always.

May we walk with you and
follow your way of love.

Help us to pick up the crosses
in our lives and
journey toward new life in you.

May we be people of prayer
in all things.

Help us to share
what we have with others.

May we turn away from selfishness
toward the light of your love.

Amen.

Action Rhyme

Action rhymes help to involve young children in learning. The following action rhyme helps children learn essential lessons about Lent.

You say the words and demonstrate the actions. The children repeat the words and imitate the actions.

Lent is a time to grow in faith	(crouch and straighten up)
and remember to pray.	(fold hands in prayer)
Lent is a season to care about others	(hands on heart)
in all we do and say.	(nod head)
Lent is a time to walk in peace	(walk in place)
along Jesus' way.	(point to each palm)
Lent is a season to listen to God	(hands cup ears)
and get ready for Easter day.	(raise arms over head)

As this activity does not require reading, it is very suitable for young children.

Cross Prayer

A cross prayer is written by students on special cross-shaped stationary. Before class make the outline of a large cross on a sheet of paper. Inside the cross piece include writing lines. At the top of the page (not in the cross) put the words "My Lent Prayer." Duplicate one copy of the cross for each child.

Remind the students that the season of Lent is a time of conversion and prayer. Then ask the children to write their own individual lenten prayers on the cross stationery. These prayers can be petitions to the Lord for strength to keep lenten promises, praise for gifts already received, or thankfulness for the Lord's gift of life and his death on our behalf.

Butterfly Cross

A butterfly is a symbol of new and transformed life. A cross is a sign of our salvation. A butterfly cross helps students understand that Easter is the fulfillment of Lent. Make a large (four to six feet in height) wooden cross and place it in the classroom or hallway throughout Lent as a symbol of the season.

During the week after Easter when you are in class, have the students decorate and add butterflies to the cross as a sign that we have new life with Jesus Christ. Resist the urge to do this during Holy Week and predate Easter.

For this activity run off a variety of brightly-colored butterfly shapes. Cut the shapes and have the students decorate their butterflies with marker or crayon drawings. Also have the students print their names someplace on the butterflies. Show the children how to fold the wings of the butterfly forward for a three dimensional effect. Have the students place their colorful butterflies on the front of the cross using double-sided tape.

The butterfly cross should remain up throughout the Easter season as a reminder that all of us share in the resurrection of Jesus Christ.

Living the Easter Season

The fifty days of Easter are a time to live in the joy of the resurrection. It is a time to celebrate new life and all that God has done for us. Keep Easter alive well past Easter Sunday. Share ideas like the following with the students for living the Easter season.

- Pray each day.
- Help someone in need.
- Give a toy to a children's shelter.
- Thank God for all your blessings.
- Make a paper butterfly to attach to a mirror.
- Read Psalm 95:1-7 ("A Call to Praise and Obedience").
- Offer each day to God.
- Be nice to someone you don't normally get along with.
- Be a peacemaker.
- Learn a new prayer.
- Play a game with a younger child.
- Read the story of Emmaus in Luke 24:13-35.
- Say the Glory Be prayer.
- Donate food to a food pantry.
- Pray for victims of violence in our world.
- Ask the Holy Spirit to guide your life.

Invite the students to think of more ideas to share. Encourage all the students to put one or more of these ideas into practice during the Easter season.

Jelly Bean Prayer

Family members of all ages are encouraged to do this Easter season project at home together. They are to fill plastic Easter eggs with jelly beans and copies of the Jelly Bean Prayer rolled up tight. These eggs can be given out at an Easter party for children in need or at any occasion when children gather during the Easter season.

Jelly Bean Prayer

RED is for the blood he gave
GREEN is for the grass he made
YELLOW is for the sun so bright
ORANGE is for the edge of night
BLACK is for the sins we made
WHITE is for the life he gave
PURPLE is for his hour of sorrow
PINK is for a new tomorrow

Remind families to fill the plastic eggs with one jelly bean of each color as included in the prayer. This is a great way to teach the essential Christian message to children in a fun way!

Alleluia Bookmark

Alleluia bookmarks with butterfly decorations will help children remember that Easter is a season of resurrection and new life. The recommended bookmark size is two inches by six inches.

In calligraphy or fancy computer font, print the words "Jesus is risen" and "Alleluia" in large type running down the page. Between "risen" and "Alleluia" put a clip art butterfly or a butterfly sticker.

Print the bookmarks on card stock of any desired color. Cut each bookmark apart. Laminate or cover the bookmarks so that they will last a long time. Put the Alleluia bookmarks in a basket and give one to each child at the end of class.

Easter Scripture Stories

Share stories of Jesus' resurrection with the students by reading or having them read aloud some of the following Bible accounts. Some are accounts of the empty tomb and others tell about the appearances of the risen Christ to his followers. If you have the students do the reading, make sure that each person has the same version of the Bible.

Mary Magdalene	Matthew 28:1-10
Make disciples	Matthew 28:16-20
Women at the tomb	Mark 16:1-8
Mary Magdalene	Mark 16:9-11
Proclaim the gospel	Mark 16:14-16
Empty tomb	Luke 24:1-12
Journey to Emmaus	Luke 24:13-35
Disciples	Luke 24:36-49
At the tomb	John 20:1-10
Mary Magdalene	John 20:11-18
Peace I leave you	John 20:19-23
Doubting Thomas	John 20:24-31
Jesus on the shore	John 21:1-14
Jesus and Peter	John 21:15-19

After each reading, take time to discuss it with the children to ascertain their understanding.

Hope Banner

The butterfly has long been an Easter symbol. As the butterfly emerges transformed from the cocoon, so Jesus has risen from death to new life. This symbol reminds us not only of the resurrection of Jesus Christ, but our own new life as Easter people.

Invite each child's family to make a butterfly at home to be displayed on a felt altar banner at the Easter season liturgies. The materials and design for the butterflies can be of each family's own choosing. Fabric, lace, felt, needlepoint, beads, and paper are some of the materials that can be used. Do furnish a butterfly pattern so that they will know what size butterfly to create. Ask the families to turn in their butterflies the week before Easter.

The felt banner should be approximately three feet by five feet. Green or blue are recommended colors. Sew a rod pocket at the top so the banner can be hung with a wooden dowel. Cut out six-inch high letters from white felt to make the words "Fill the World" at the top of the banner and "With Hope" at the bottom. Use craft glue which will not soak through the felt to connect the letters.

Pin the butterflies onto the banner in a pleasing arrangement. Hang the banner in church during a school, religious education, or Sunday liturgy during the Easter season.

Prayer for Easter

Easter is a season where all of our hopes are fulfilled. Pray this prayer of hope with your students.

Father, through the life, death, and resurrection
of your Son, Jesus Christ,
we are called to new life in the Spirit.

Transform our lives so that we may
live always as people of hope.
Enable us to share the good news to all.

May we praise you in all that we do
and live in your love.
We pray in the name of your Son, Jesus Christ.

Amen.

Memory Tree

The loss of a classmate or family member leaves children and others feeling helpless. One way to help those who are dealing with loss is by planting a memory tree.

Contact the families of the people who have died and are to be remembered. Ask their permission to plant a memory tree. Invite them to the planting at a specific day and time. Plant one or more small trees on parish or school grounds.

Gather the children, families, and teachers for a prayer and a scripture reading followed by the planting of the trees. An appropriate song—one that the children know—can also be sung. An individual plaque giving the name of the person who has died should be engraved professional-ly and attached to a brick near the planted tree.

When the children and others pass by these trees, they are comforted because they know that their loved ones are remembered. The buds and leaves on the trees each spring remind all of us that death is not the end, but a beginning of new life with God.

Pentecost Ideas

This activity helps to foster an awareness of the presence of the Holy Spirit in our lives and in the lives of others. The Holy Spirit can be difficult for children to understand. We must make it more concrete. The time near the feast of Pentecost is an opportune time.

By focusing on the signs of the Spirit in our world, we can help children begin to understand the role of the Spirit in our lives. We know that the Holy Spirit is at work in our world when:

- people bring in food for those in need.
- one child helps another with homework.
- a community reaches out to a family after a fire.
- an older sister reads a story to a younger brother.
- one person prays for the needs of another.
- a family helps another family cope with the loss of a loved one.
- people praise God together at Mass.

Invite the children to contribute ideas to the discussion of times when we see the actions of the Holy Spirit in our world.

Spirit Promise

On Pentecost, the Holy Spirit came to be with the church. Discuss with the students what it means to live as people guided by the Holy Spirit. Have the children sign a promise to be open to the Holy Spirit in their lives. In this way they will remember that we are to live in the Spirit of God.

Before class prepare the Spirit Promise sheets as below.

Inside the outline of a dove print the title "Living in the Spirit." Below the title print the words "I will be open to the Holy Spirit in my life." Provide a blank line for the children to sign their names. Duplicate the Spirit Promises two to a page. Cut them out and give one to each child.

After the children sign their Spirit Promise, have them take it home as a visible reminder to live always in the Spirit of God.

Holy Spirit Chain

It is important for children to learn to address prayers to the Holy Spirit for guidance, as well as to God the Father and to Jesus. A ten-link paper chain with a traditional Holy Spirit prayer can help them learn to pray to the Holy Spirit. Duplicate on red and white paper each word of the following prayer. Then cut them apart as one-inch strips.

> Come Holy Spirit,
> direct my every thought,
> word, and action.

The children assemble the chain in the order of the words of the prayer. Tell them to alternate red and white links in their chain, and connect them with tape.

This activity encourages the children to learn and memorize a prayer to the Holy Spirit. It is especially appropriate around the time of Pentecost.

6
Celebrating Special Days

Many special feast days and holidays are celebrated throughout the church year.

Some of the special days we observe are the feasts and memorials of saints. The struggles of saints mirror our own. Saints show us how to deal with these struggles and how to love God and reach out to people in need along the way. The saints are with us on our journey with Jesus. All of us are called to be saintly and to live the gospel each day. It is also a tradition in our church to ask the saints to intercede for us with God. Many lessons build on this practice.

Through the special days and celebrations on the church calendar we acknowledge God as the Creator of all people and remember that we are to give praise to God. These special days remind us of God's presence in our lives and in the world. They call us to share the good news with all.

Birthday Party for Mary

September 8 is the feast of the birth of the Virgin Mary. Have a birthday party on or near September 8 to honor Mary. Call on parents to provide cupcakes and juice for the children.

Before the food is shared, give a short talk on the life and faithful example of Mary. Explain the significance of Mary's response of "yes" to the angel's request that she be the Mother of God. Sing a round of "Happy Birthday" to Mary. Then serve the food and drinks.

It's important to always honor Mary. What better time to begin than her birthday? The party also helps build a sense of community among the children at the beginning of the school year.

Story of St. Thérèse

We observe the memorial of St. Thérèse, the Little Flower, on October 1. Share the following story about the life of this humble and much beloved saint. Use the questions in italics to begin a dialogue between you and the children. Call on volunteers to respond.

St. Thérèse was the youngest child in her family. *Are any of you the youngest in your family?* Then you are like her. She lived in France. She is sometimes called St. Thérèse of Lisieux because that is the name of her hometown. Her older sisters became nuns. She also became a Carmelite nun when she was only 15 years old.

Thérèse showed her love for God by trying to do her best each day in everything she did. She was a simple person, and she once described herself as the Little Flower.

She is an example of how to be holy in everyday life. She trusted God in all things. *Do you sometimes have to do chores?* St. Thérèse had to do chores around the convent every day. She scrubbed floors and did laundry.

St. Thérèse offered everything she did to God. *Was someone critical of you, but you did not yell at them?* Then you are like St. Thérèse. She did not speak unkindly to others. She tried very hard to do what was expected of her even when things were not fair. You can try to be like her.

St. Thérèse kept a journal. *Did you ever write down how you felt in a diary?* This is like what St. Thérèse did. She wrote down her memories and her feelings. She wrote how she tried to do God's will even in small things. Everything she did each day she offered to God. Sometimes it was a struggle for her. Her written words were later published as a book called *The Story of a Soul.*

Thérèse prayed to God from her heart. *Do you talk to God in your own words?* She prayed for the needs of others. She prayed especially for the missionaries. She is now known as the Patroness of Missions. *Do you pray for the intentions of other people besides just yourself?* That is what Thérèse did.

Thérèse was often sick. *What was the worst illness you ever had?* Then you know how badly she must have felt sometimes. But she tried not to complain. She died of tuberculosis at the age of 24. Thérèse promised to spend her time in heaven doing good for people on earth. We can live like St. Thérèse if we try to do our best each day.

Prayer of St. Francis

We celebrate the life of St. Francis on October 4. The Prayer of St. Francis speaks to us of the kind of people we should be and how we are to live in peace. This prayer is a guide for living.

Discuss each of the elements of the Prayer of St. Francis with the children. Then teach them to pray this prayer using the accompanying gestures.

Prayer of St. Francis

Lord, make me an instrument of your peace
where there is hatred, let me bring love
(stretch out arms)

where there is injury, let me bring pardon
(brush hand over upturned palm)

where there is doubt, let me bring faith
(hands together in prayer)

where there is despair, let me bring hope
(hands over heart)

where there is darkness, let me bring light
(with palms up, move hands apart)

and where there is sadness, let me bring joy.
(raise joined hands upward)

This prayer reminds us that we are to live as people of forgiveness and peace. It helps us learn to live as followers of Jesus Christ following the example of St. Francis.

Living Rosary

The living rosary is a wonderful devotion that honors Mary. This can be done on or near the memorial of Our Lady of the Rosary on October 7 or any time during the month of May. The living rosary is held in the church, hall, or outdoors. Ideally, sixty children are needed to form the complete circular shape of the rosary beads (around a statue of Mary) though the living rosary can be adapted with fewer children.

The living rosary begins with a Marian hymn. The children process forward during the opening song. Then the student representing the Apostle's Creed bead makes the sign of the cross and says the first part of the Apostle's Creed (to "I believe in the Holy Spirit"). The assembly concludes the prayer. The next student says the first part of the Our Father (to "Give us this day"). The assembly says the second part. The rosary continues with the first three beads. Each student comes forward to lead a Hail Mary ("to Holy Mary, Mother of God"). The assembly finishes the prayer.

The glorious mysteries are especially appropriate for the living rosary. The first glorious mystery is named by the student with the Our Father bead. This person may also share a related scripture passage. The ten students with the first glorious mystery beads then take their turns one by one as prayer leaders for the Hail Marys. The rosary continues in this way, the "Our Father" students introducing each of the mysteries.

Conclude with a song to honor Mary.

All Saints' Day Parade

We celebrate All Saints' Day on November 1. The saints remembered on this day are those who do not have their own individual feast days. We also remember many of our deceased Christian brothers and sisters who are not officially canonized saints, but still, by virtue of their lives, are saints nonetheless.

Coming near Halloween, encourage the children to wear a saint costume in the same mode as Halloween costumes. Assign older children to research individual saints and determine elements of distinctive dress. Use props like the following to help distinguish the saints:

- a rosary for Mary
- a silk rose for Thérèse
- a large paper shamrock for St. Patrick
- a hammer for St. Joseph
- a school book for St. Elizabeth Seton
- a basket of food for St. Vincent de Paul

One at a time have the children come to the front of the classroom and tell the other children what saint they are representing and what they learned about the saint. Allow them to use note cards if needed.

Learning by doing involves the students in the lesson. Because they took an active role, the students are more likely to remember the meaning of All Saints' Day and the saint they portrayed.

Saints on the Way

Another important part of our All Saints' Day observance on November 1 is to stress with the children that all of us are called to be saints. Through our baptism each of us is called to life with God. Each of us is created in God's image and likeness. We are to live the life for which we were created by God.

Discuss with the children how they can be holy. Suggest ways they can follow Jesus in their daily lives, like:

- praying for the needs of others.
- bringing canned goods to the parish food pantry.
- stepping in when someone is mean to another child.
- praising God by actively participating in Sunday Mass.
- forgiving someone who has hurt you.
- offering each day to God.
- donating part of your allowance to Catholic Relief Services.

Allow the children to come up with other ideas on their own. We are all to aspire to holiness each day. That is how we can become saints!

Models of Faith

Besides well-known canonized saints, children need examples of modern day people who follow the challenge of the gospel. Share practical examples of people in your own community who help others. These can be from personal experience, or taken from magazine or newspaper articles. You can have a person come and speak with the class. Consider the following:

Literacy volunteers teach English to refugees from war-torn nations or other new immigrants to the United States.

Doctors, nurses and dentists use their vacation time to go to poor countries. They give free medical and dental care to those who desperately need it. They make it possible for children to have physical defects corrected and for adults to receive the dental care they need. Many times this type of care is not available in underdeveloped countries.

Volunteers at homeless shelters and soup kitchens make and serve meals. They give of their time each week or each month so that people in need will have a nourishing meal to eat when they are hungry.

Habitat for Humanity volunteers build houses for people of low income. Those for whom the house is being built also help with the actual construction.

Hospice volunteers work with adults and children who are dying. They give aid and comfort to those who need it. They also minister to family members of the dying.

Volunteer trainers train dogs to help people with disabilities. These dogs can pick up dropped items and bring things to the person they serve. In this way people with physical disabilities are able to live independently.

These people make a difference in our world and in the lives of others. Share the example of how they put their faith into action.

All Souls Memory Book

All Souls' Day is observed on November 2. We remember in a special way those who have died. This is a day when children are comforted to know that we do not forget family members and friends who have gone before us.

Make a memory book in a three-ringed binder for All Souls' Day in which children can write the names of deceased relatives and friends and anyone else they know who has died. This helps the children understand that their loved ones are not forgotten.

For the cover of the binder, print "All Souls' Day" and "November 2" with a cross in the middle. Slip the cover into the front of the binder with a see-through cover. On the top of a blank page, put the words "We pray for those who have died." At the bottom of the page, include Jesus' words, "I am the resurrection and the life." The space in between should be left blank for the students to write the names of their deceased loved ones.

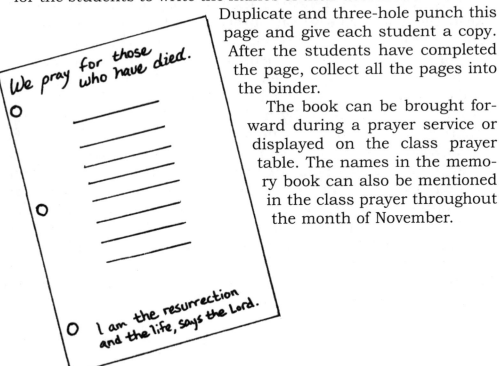

Duplicate and three-hole punch this page and give each student a copy. After the students have completed the page, collect all the pages into the binder.

The book can be brought forward during a prayer service or displayed on the class prayer table. The names in the memory book can also be mentioned in the class prayer throughout the month of November.

Followers of Jesus Role Play

The church celebrates St. Andrew with a feast day on November 30. St. Andrew is the brother of St. Peter. With Peter, he left everything behind to follow Jesus while fishing on Lake Galilee. This story of the call of the first disciples is found in Matthew 4:18-22. Read the story to the children from the Bible.

Next, invite the students to pantomime the story as you read again. Choose six characters for the major roles:

Jesus
Peter
Andrew
James
John
Zebedee

Have the actors rehearse their actions before performing. Read the words slowly. Encourage the students to improvise, and be dramatic in role playing the actions of the scene.

For example, the scene opens with the children pretending to be fishermen pulling in their nets. Then Jesus walks by and stands by the first two fishermen. Peter and Andrew look up. Jesus beckons to them by motioning with his arm. Peter and Andrew then "drop" their nets behind and follow him. Next, Jesus walks over to James and John and calls them to follow. They put down their nets and follow Jesus. Zebedee waves good-bye as Jesus and the four apostles keep walking to the other side of the "stage." Remember, encourage improvisation!

Repeat the play allowing other students the chance to be actors. Discuss the meaning of the story with the entire class: We leave everything behind in order to follow Jesus. The example of St. Andrew is a reminder to do God's will in our lives and to always follow Jesus.

Valentine Luncheon for Older Adults

Valentine's Day is a perfect holiday to remind children of the opportunities to share God's love with others.

Arrange for the students to help with a luncheon on the Sunday before Valentine's Day for older adults (age sixty-five plus) in the parish. The older people will appreciate being able to attend lunch after morning Mass without having to venture out after dark.

Junior high students can be responsible for serving the meal.

Younger children can make Valentine's Day party favors. Show the students how to cut out a red heart shape and glue a candy cup in the middle. They can decorate the heart with stickers and fill the cup with "conversation hearts." These favors look great on the tables and are much appreciated by the older adults.

Love One Another Bookmarks

The challenge of the gospel is that we are to love and care about all people, not just those who are easy to love. The time surrounding Valentine's Day is a good chance to emphasize this teaching with children.

A gift for children that will remind them to love others is a bookmark with this good news printed out. These bookmarks feature the scripture verse from John 15:12:

Love one another as I love you.

Use a computer to print the verse on the page in large, red ink. In between "Love one another" and "as I love you" put a heart for illustration. A recommended size for the bookmark is two inches by six inches. Duplicate on white cardstock and laminate the bookmarks.

Challenge the children to live the verse from John 5:12 and to care for all people.

Irish Blessing

St. Patrick's Day is an opportune time to share a traditional Irish blessing with the children. Type or write this prayer inside the outline of a large shamrock. Duplicate them onto green paper, and distribute a copy to each person. After praying the words, allow the children to share about how God has blessed their lives; how God has shined the warm sun upon their faces.

Irish Blessing

As you go with Christ:
May the road rise up to meet you,
May the wind be always at your back,
May the sun shine warm upon your face,
The rains fall soft upon your fields,
And, until we meet again,
May God hold you in the palm of his hand.

Mary Litany

The Annunciation of the Lord is on March 25, nine months before Christmas. This is the day we celebrate Mary's "yes" to the angel Gabriel that she would be the Mother of God. We too are called to be faithful to God's will. We too are to allow the Holy Spirit to work in our lives.

Let the children know that we can call on Mary and the other saints and ask them to pray for us. Use the following litany to honor Mary and ask for her prayers. Lead the prayer yourself or call on children to read the various parts.

> Mary, faithful person,
>> pray for us.
> Mary, woman of prayer,
>> pray for us.
> Mary, mother of our Lord,
>> pray for us.
> Mary, full of grace,
>> pray for us.
> Mary, loving mother,
>> pray for us.
> Mary, trusting person,
>> pray for us.
> Mary, bearer of hope,
>> pray for us.
> Mary, queen of heaven,
>> pray for us.

By praying a Mary litany together, we encourage children to honor Mary. In this way devotion to Mary is handed on to another generation of believers.

May Crowning

May is the traditional "month of Mary." A familiar Mary custom is the "crowning of Mary" in which a crown of flowers is placed on the head of a Mary statue in the church, outside of the church, or anywhere a statue of Mary is placed. The following suggestions for a May crowning ceremony can be adapted or expanded depending on the situation and group involved.

Introduction. Begin with remarks about the reasons why we honor Mary, the Mother of God.

Opening Song. Sing together a traditional Mary song such as "Immaculate Mary."

Gospel Reading. Share a gospel reading of the Magnificat (Luke 1:46-50). This is a reading in which Mary praises God for all God has done for her.

Procession. The children process two by two to lay fresh flowers they have brought from home into a basket at the foot of the statute of Mary. During this procession instrumental music is played.

Crowning. The one student who has been chosen to crown the statue of Mary comes forward and places a flower crown on the head of the statue. If the statue of Mary being crowned has Mary holding Jesus in her arms, then a crown must first be placed on the Son, then on the Mother of the Son of God. If desired, a statue of Joseph can be crowned at the same time by another child to honor the holy family.

Prayer. After the crowning all can join in praying a Mary litany prayer, Hail Mary, or another Marian prayer.

Closing Song. Sing together "Hail Holy Queen" or another appropriate song with a Marian theme.

In this way we honor Mary for listening to the word of God in her life and for being an example of faith. A May crowning allows the students to participate in a devotion that has been a custom for generations of believers.

Endnotes

Chapter 2

Peacemaking Actions is adapted from James McGinnis, *Educating for Peace and Justice: Religious Dimensions, K-6* (St. Louis, MO: Institute for Peace and Justice, 1993), pp. 16-17.

Family Service Day is an idea shared from St. Cecilia Catholic Community in Houston.

Forgiveness Chain is from *Welcome to the Family* (Allen, TX: Resources for Christian Living, 1999), p. 146.

Chapter 3

Awareness Activity is adapted from the Columban Fathers' *Teaching Global Awareness* mission program.

Chapter 4

Advent Story is from *Kid Collection: Resources for Cycle B* (Liguori, MO: Liguori Publications,1995), cd rom. www.liguori.org

Chapter 5

Hope Banner is from *Extra Help for Sunday School Teachers* (St. Louis: Concordia Publishing House, 1994). Used with permission under license number 99: 8-95.